HOLY SPIRIT UNLOCK THE PATH FORWARD

The Steps to Living a Life of
Purpose and Fulfillment

Janice Rhodes Casey

―――――

HOLY SPIRIT
UNLOCK THE PATH
FORWARD

―――――

The Steps to Living a Life of
Purpose and Fulfillment

Dedication

I want to thank my husband, Darrell Casey, my best friend, for your constant support and encouragement. Your story is my story. I am ever so blessed that God connected us. My love for you is forever. To our children—Darrell, Steven, Jordan, Jennifer, Dorrian, and your families and especially our grandchildren, you are my inspiration for passing the baton with faith, decency, and integrity. I love all of you guys so much.

ACKNOWLEDGMENTS

Thank you to my sister, Joyce, my brother, Hubert, and all my nieces, especially my triplets—flower girls Tish and Nikki and my ring bearer, Christy, to my nephews, in-laws, and cousins. You are all so special to me. I am blessed to have such an amazing family. To my mom, Jennie R. Rhodes, thank you for your tenacity, independence, and creativity. You are my forever teacher. Thank you for showing me how to step out on faith. To my wonderful dad, King Edward Rhodes, Sr., and my intelligent brothers Preston and King, all of whom are resting in their heavenly homes, thank you for showing me how to be innovative and loving at the same time.

Thank you:

- Dee Greene for introducing me to the possibilities of social media for reaching the Kingdom of God.

- Donald, Pat, and Amy, for your invaluable feedback.

- Chanel, Lindsey, Nakeisa, Chandler, and John, for the awesome fresh word in Prophetic Planning for Your Day every day that has kept me motivated.

- Wendy P. for teaching me about the power of God's Holy Spirit.

- Dr. Monique and Jasmine, for your encouragement, teachings, and your push to finish this book with excellence.

- Ramesha Nicole for helping me get rid of some unnecessary weight that was holding me back.

- All of you at Beyond the Book Media, including Monique and Jacinta.

All Glory, Honor, and Praise goes to the Father, Son, and Holy Spirit without whom none of this would exist.

TABLE OF CONTENTS

INTRODUCTION

When I accepted Jesus Christ as my Lord and Savior, I was nine years old. I remember hearing the simple, straightforward explanation of the gospel at a church camp and watching an old reel-to-reel movie about the life of Jesus Christ. It was touching and convicting. That night, along with several other campers, I gave Jesus my life.

During the week-long camp, we had to memorize a scripture a day. John 3:16, Romans 3:23, Isaiah 26:3 were three of them that have stuck with me for a lifetime. Two songs that we sang at that camp also stuck with me—I Have Decided to Follow Jesus and He's Able. There were young teenage girls there that served as camp counselors. One of them, Debbie Bordeau, and I shared letters and kept in touch for years after camp—through her high school graduation and her college graduation from a school in Canada, her marriage to Dave Wright, their life in Arizona, and then finally through her move back to Bradenton, Florida. At that time, we stopped all correspondence for whatever reason, but the indelible mark of her Christian discipleship had been tattooed on me. Her father had been one of the Pastors at the camp, and their kindness made a difference. I was a lone 9-year-old black girl at that rural camp in South Georgia in 1969.

During those years of correspondence with Debbie, we shared our faith and our hopes and desires. Her Godly wisdom and fierce faith greatly impacted my life, as did the memories of that week-long camp near a lake outside of Valdosta, GA. Those activities and memories, coupled with growing up in a Christian home and being active in my church, formed the foundation of my walk with Christ. But even though I had that foundation, my life has been full of twists and turns, trials and errors, and mistakes and merits. Navigating the twists and turns of life has not been easy. Sometimes it has been downright frustrating and disappointing, but I have grown immensely in my walk with Christ through it all.

Now I have the opportunity and privilege to make an impact on the lives of others. Here, I share important scriptures and how they apply to your life. I share how to unlock the path forward in your Christian journey to having a full and purposeful life. This book is a compilation of what I have learned about the importance of prayer and being led by the Holy Spirit. It speaks of ways to activate your faith, how to prepare to leave treasured legacies, and most importantly, how to stay focused on Jesus. It opens the door and allows you to peek inside and see a transformed life that you, too, can have through a realistic step-by-step approach. *Holy Spirit, Unlock the Path Forward.*

PART I

PRAY IN ALL HONESTY

Always Begin with Prayer

CHAPTER I

UNLOCK THE PATH

If you abide in My word, you are My disciples indeed.
And you shall know the truth, and the truth shall make you free.

- John 8:31b-32

One of the greatest joys of parenthood is when your baby first says mama or daddy. There is just that special connection that you feel when they learn to communicate with you and affirm you as their source of strength and as their advocate—the one they depend on for nourishment and life itself. As they get older and can communicate what their needs are, what hurts them, and what they enjoy, parents are so grateful for this connection.

Imagine that our Heavenly Father feels the very same way. He enjoys the communication with His children. He has given us prayer as the ordained way for us to reach out to Him and tell Him what our needs and desires are. We can tell Him in prayer what hurts us and ask Him for what we need and want. Then we listen for His answers by turning ourselves inward to the Spirit of God.

In the early years of my marriage, I often employed the silent treatment, neither speaking nor listening, in order to get what I wanted or to get my point across. I soon found out that while it was often wise to stop talking too much, it was not smart to stop listening. By listening to my husband, I often realized that was where my understanding manifested. I gained perspective and wisdom. Prayer is the same, where you are talking to and then listening to hear from God. A wise man once said that is why God gave us one mouth and two ears. We must listen twice as much as we talk.

We must listen to the leading and wisdom of His Holy Spirit. We must spend dedicated time with God daily. Talk to God, especially about His Word, and then listen for reaction and guidance. You may say, just how do I listen for God's answers. We listen in a myriad of ways. Remember when Elijah was waiting to hear from God in I Kings 19. God was not in the wind or the earthquake but in the small still voice. God may be an audible voice speaking to you, or you may hear Him through the study of His Word. He may be in a song, a sermon, a book, or in a conversation. God can speak to you in a dream, an idea, or in nature. Your job is to be alert and in an attitude of expectation that His answers will come. Ask questions, state your opinions, dreams, and aspirations. Tell God about your worries and concerns. Even say when you are angry with Him. David did so quite often, but his anger often turned into joyful praise as he was reminded of God's goodness. At all the stages of life, the teen years, during motherhood or fatherhood, during your working years, and beyond, there are distractions that make time with God hard to accomplish. However, it is a must if we are going to enjoy life to the fullest. Remember, we don't enjoy relationships with others without communicating with them. And we do not enjoy our saved lives without communicating with God. We must seek Him in prayer. When we stop treating God like some big, untouchable entity in the sky and we bring Him into our space as our confidante and trusted ally, we allow Him the right to advocate for us. As freewill agents, we can deny God. Without realizing it, sometimes we are denying Him. We do so when we dismiss His presence in our daily lives. We think we are being reverent to Him, but we are really closing Him out. God wants to communicate with us, to help us, to tell us which way to turn, when to go forward and when to stop. He wants access to us, but He will not boggart His way into our lives. He will only come if we invite Him.

The Bible records how important prayer time was to Jesus. He made a deliberate effort to spend time with God. He prayed early mornings, late nights, before and after great events, and when life was especially busy and trying. "If Jesus, who is the Savior of the World, the sinless Son of God, thought it worthwhile to clear His calendar to pray, wouldn't it be wise for us to do the same?" (Lucado, 2007)

So, when we talk about truth or consequences, we must consider that there will be unfavorable consequences when we are not communicating with God. "As long as prayer remains an afterthought, a formality, a mindless mix of duty and manipulation, something we do but usually don't do, and rarely if ever do with any meaning and vitality, with confidence and clarity," nothing will change (Nicole, 2021). When we refuse to pray to Him and ask for His forgiveness of our sins, when we refuse to repent of ungodliness, when we refuse to acknowledge God as the head of our life, the enemy comes. The goal of Satan and his demons is to steal, kill, and destroy. He is your enemy and not your friend. I hear some of you saying that you can avoid those consequences because you can steer clear of bad people and influences. The reality is that you need to wear the full armor of God daily because we wrestle not with mere humans but against principalities, powers, rulers of darkness, and spiritual wickedness in the heavenly realms. Ephesians 6 reminds us that we wrestle largely against an unseen, invisible enemy. In addition to putting on the armor of God, we must always pray with all prayer and supplication in the Spirit. Praying in the Spirit means we enter the mindset of Christ. As we speak to God, whether using our Holy Spirit prayer language or our native tongue, we are fully engaging a mind that stays on God and His agenda, not ours. As Jesus prayed in the garden just before going to the cross, His prayer was so transparent. He said, "God, I do not want to do this hard thing. I wish there was some other way, but since I know this is what you have ordained, then I put aside my desire, and I take up Your Will as mine. Let Your Will be done!" How powerful is that?!

You may say, "I am praying daily, but still I am overwhelmed by life and stuck in a bad place. What do I do? Why does this seem to happen over and over?" Let me suggest that even if you are communicating with God through prayer, that your prayers are not being fully honest with God. Often, they are mere superficial attempts at connecting with God, like checking an item off your to-do list. John 8:32 says, "the truth will make us free." What is really going on that is keeping you in bondage, that is holding you back, that is not allowing you to live the abundant life?

It was during a Bible study lesson that I realized that I was indeed practicing image management (Free of Me Bible Study, 2018). I was trying to put forth the image of someone who has it all together when really, I was largely overwhelmed, often insecure, and in need of validation. When challenged on letting that go and being vulnerable, I reached a new level of freedom to love God and allow His confirmation to sustain me. Let go of the trauma that is keeping you from reaching freedom and peace in your life, and you will be amazed at how your journey is transformed.

Maybe your problem is not image management. Maybe you are dealing with unforgiveness. Remember that Jesus said in Matthew 5:23-24 that "if you bring a gift to Him but have an issue with your brother, you must leave your gift. First, go and be reconciled with your brother and then come and offer your gift." Unforgiveness robs you of time and comfort. It strips you of blessings that could occur in your life. God does not honor your prayers when you harbor enmity in your heart. Perhaps you feel justified in your behavior. Maybe the person violated you in some way, abused, neglected, or mistreated you. Forgiveness is not excusing the wrong that they did to you, but rather it is letting go of the power they hold over you. You may not realize it, but many poor decisions that you make or have made were made because of the issue you have with the person(s) you have not forgiven. This includes many bad financial decisions. You may think you have moved on, but really you are hiding the truth inside. Psalm 51:6, David had to admit to God that God's desire is the truth that is inside of us. "Behold, You desire truth in the inward parts, and in the hidden part You will make me to know wisdom."

When we are truthful with God, He will show us how to fix the problem. So be quick to repent of known sins. Empty out the shame and guilt that you feel. Admit to God that your sins still haunt you. Remember, Jesus knows all about shame. He bore the shame of the cross just for you. Now you will need to forgive yourself and allow God's peace to fill your heart. Transparency with God is key. He won't help you with what you will not admit. Wisely, that is the first rule of Alcoholics Anonymous. You must first acknowledge that you have a problem. Take it to God in prayer, all of it. Even the fears that you harbor must be admitted.

When I felt God tugging on my heart to work in ministry, I was terrified because I was not a confident public speaker. Even though, as a teacher, I had no problems dealing with a classroom full of students, I was very afraid and uncomfortable addressing my teacher colleagues in a meeting or at other gatherings. I avoided doing activities at work that required any public speaking. I, like Moses, admitted to God that I did not speak well. I wasn't confident. I did not think I could do it. But God is persistent, and I acknowledged my call into ministry despite my fears. As God began to heal me of the image management that I persisted in, I began to focus more and more on His power and authority. By focusing on Him and speaking aloud, "It's not about me, God, but all about You," the intimidation I felt about public speaking began to drop off. I no longer harbor over-the-top concerns about how I look or whether I am doing everything perfectly, but I am representing a greater source than me. I am representing God, and He is speaking through me. I am just an instrument, but I first realized this in my prayer life by speaking God's Words back to Him.

Another thing I realized as I began to grow in my relationship with God was that because I represent someone greater, I must be open to relationships with others. Rather than being exclusive of others, especially those who do not look like me, I make a point to be inclusive, seeing that we are all God's children and deserve love and respect, despite our differences. I have been in many circumstances when one person included me in the conversation or activities. Just that one person made the difference in my ability to function in that setting. We must be willing to do the same for others. We should not get in positions of authority for ourselves but to make a way for others. In John 2, we are told that "Jesus was invited to the wedding in Cana." The disciples were able to go because they were with Jesus. That's how they gained access. Sometimes others get access only because of you. Know that God expects us to help others to gain access to Him and His blessings. We are to pray intercessory prayers for others, standing in the gap for them. Most of us pray for ourselves, our families, and those we know. We are also commanded to pray for other people, especially those in authority over us and those who do not know the Lord. Praying without ceasing literally means that we continue an ongoing conversation with God about all things.

So, the question is, are we praying to God, and are we praying in all honesty? Are we having conversations with God daily about the details of our lives? Are we praying and listening for answers to the issues of life? Have we come clean about our sins and repented of all of them, even the ones we still want to hide from? Are we praying for those around the world in every area of society? The reality is that we need to pray in all honesty about everything that concerns us, the good and the bad.

Questions to Ponder

1. Am I in tune with the voice of God because I have regular communication with Him?

2. Do I allow Him access to all of me and my concerns?

3. When I pray, do I consider others and their needs?

4. Is prayer the first or last thing that I think of before moving forward?

CHAPTER II

OBEDIENCE TO THE HOLY SPIRIT

Do not cast me away from Your presence,

And do not take Your Holy Spirit from me.

- Psalm 51:11

Now that we realize what a privilege it is to have regular prayer time with God, let's talk about the power of prayer. Remember, the real power of prayer is that it helps us live out our lives with passion and purpose. But the power comes not from merely what we say in our prayer time. The power comes from activating the leading of God's Holy Spirit over our lives.

Often, talk of the third person of the Trinity, the Holy Spirit, evokes strong emotion. Either people strongly discount the need of the Holy Spirit in their lives, or they strongly desire the constant presence of Him. Some declare like the disciples in Ephesus who said to Paul that they had not even heard about a Holy Spirit. Jesus Himself gave important information concerning the Holy Spirit at the beginning of the book of Acts. Jesus, when assembled with his chosen apostles and believers, just prior to ascending back into the heavens, gave these instructions:

> "for John truly baptized with water, but you shall be baptized
> with the Holy Spirit not many days from now... But you shall
> receive power when the Holy Spirit has come upon you; and
> you shall be witnesses to Me in Jerusalem, and in all Judea and
> Samaria, and to the end of the earth." Acts 1:5,8

Some days later, after they returned to Jerusalem, when they were all in agreement and praying in the upper room on the day of Pentecost, the Holy Spirit descended on all 120 of them. They heard a sound coming down from heaven like a mighty rushing wind that filled the whole house. Then something like fire appeared to each of them, and one sat on each of them. They all began to speak in other languages as the Holy Spirit gave them utterance. All the people of the various nations of the world who were in Jerusalem were confused because everyone heard someone speak in their own language. That's when Peter came out to explain that they were not drunk because it was only 9:00 in the morning but what had occurred was the fulfillment of the prophecy of Joel that said in the last days that God would pour out His Spirit on all flesh. Your sons and daughters will prophesy, which means to tell of things to come.

And just as Jesus had promised, the Holy Spirit gave them the power to do phenomenal things. Because of His leading and their obedience to follow, the early church grew daily. And during the times of great persecution, the church grew even more. You see, God the Father, His Son Jesus Christ, and the Holy Spirit were here from the beginning. Remember, God is an uncreated Spirit. He has always existed and will live forever. The Trinity is the concept that was given to Godly men to explain the existence of one God in three forms to accomplish different tasks. During the creation, the Word says that the Spirit of God hovered over the face of the waters. God spoke, and the Holy Spirit used His power to accomplish the task of creation. During the Old Testament, we see the Spirit of God descending upon men at various times to accomplish God's purposes. Samson was filled with the Spirit when he killed an army of men with the jawbone of an ass. When Samuel anointed David as King of Israel, the Spirit came upon David. Even in the beginning of the New Testament, we see the Holy Spirit accomplish various activities. He overshadowed Mary to impregnate her with Jesus. It was Holy Spirit power that raised Jesus from the dead.

There are scriptures in the gospels that indicate that the Holy Spirit was present in the lives of believers, but His role took on a new prominence following the days of Pentecost to accomplish the continued growth of the ministry of Jesus Christ. We have come to realize that the same power of the Holy Spirit that raised Jesus Christ from the dead lives in all who give their lives to Christ. When we accept Christ as our personal Savior, the Holy Spirit comes to reside in us. Sometimes we discount Him by identifying His leading as 'my mind told me, or something told me' rather than crediting God's Spirit with the results. By observing this power and being obedient to the leading of the Holy Spirit, we maintain continuous access to God's power.

However, the Holy Spirit is not merely a source of power and energy as some sects have described Him. Like God the Father and His Son, Jesus, the

Holy Spirit has a personality. He has intellect, emotion, wisdom, and willpower. Various scriptures refer to His personality.

- Apostle Paul in 1 Corinthians 2:11 notes the intellectual ability of the Holy Spirit.

- Romans 15:30 speaks of the love of the Holy Spirit.

- Ephesians. 4:30 speaks of grieving the Holy Spirit.

- 1 Corinthians 12:11 speaks of His ability to give spiritual gifts, including the gift of tongues. (Theology for Today, 2002)

Many early Christians recognized and affirmed the Holy Spirit as a person and were obedient to His leading.

- Peter obeyed the Holy Spirit when he was commanded to go to Cornelius's household in Acts 10:19.

- Ananias went to Paul, having been directed by the Spirit in Acts 9:10-17.

- Paul and Silas were led by the Holy Spirit in ministry in Acts 16. (Theology for Today, 2002)

Note that there are warnings given in the Bible to acknowledge the important work of the Holy Spirit in our lives.

- Jesus warned of blasphemy of the Holy Spirit in Matthew 12:31.

- The Bible warns of the consequences of insulting the Holy Spirit in Hebrews 10:29.

- We should have the proper reverence of the person of the Holy Spirit as did David in Psalm 51:11.

- We must not attempt to lie to the Holy Spirit, as did Ananias and Saphira in Acts 5:1-11. (Theology for Today, 2002)

So, if we are going to move forward in the power of the Almighty, we must listen to, be led by, and follow the leading of God's Holy Spirit. We must not grieve or discount the Holy Spirit. He is the inspiration, creativity, wisdom, guidance, prophecy, and power that we need to move forward in this life. Making the mistake of discounting God's Spirit is huge, for the Word says in Zechariah 4:6, "...Not by might nor by power, but by my Spirit, says the Lord."

I have many testimonies of God's Spirit working on my behalf. I want to share one. Observe how obedience to the Holy Spirit affects our lives and not just our spiritual lives but our secular lives as well.

When I was burned out as a classroom teacher, the Holy Spirit had prompted me to begin work on a degree in media to obtain a job as a school library media specialist in the future. I had just begun the media program in June of the '90s when I found out three librarian positions were open in my district. That's odd. Those positions were usually hard to come by because most schools only employed one librarian, and most of those people kept the same position for years. As the summer wore on, I found out that two positions had been quickly filled, but one was still open.

At the end of July, I had to go to the district office to pick up my paycheck, and I knew the last position was still available. As I headed inside the building, the Holy Spirit prompted me to ask to see the personnel director before leaving, to ask for the job. I dismissed it as silly head talk since I had no degree in that area, no prior experience, and certainly no certificate. I picked up my paycheck and returned to my car. As I was backing out to leave, the Holy Spirit spoke to me again. "Go back." I stopped and pulled forward. Then I shook my head and started to back up again. This time the Holy Spirit shouted, "GO BACK!" Startled, I pulled back into the parking spot, got out, and headed towards the door. All the time, I thought that it was a stupid idea. I reached the door and opened it.

The personnel director was standing there at the desk. He turned and saw me. He said that he was just about to call me because he had heard that I was working on a library media degree. He proceeded to take me to his office, offer me the job, and had his secretary file for a 3-year temporary certificate that would give me time to complete my professional certification. In two weeks, when school began, I was the new library media specialist at Camden Middle School, all because I was obedient to the Holy Spirit. There was no earthquake, tornado, and thunder and lightning when the Holy Spirit spoke to me, but just His voice, giving me instructions. However, my obedience to Him at that moment was life-changing.

So, what is it that we really need the Holy Spirit to do for us? What are we asking Him for? We should ask for help with the decisions we need to make. We need guidance and wisdom on how to proceed forward with the normal activities of life, like getting along with others, raising our children, and making a living. We need His power to push forward with difficult tasks. And we need His comprehensive abilities to live our lives with passion and purpose. No matter how ludicrous it seems, be obedient.

Questions to Ponder:

1. Am I Spirit-led?

2. When has God made a way out of no way because I was obedient to His Holy Spirit?

3. What is stopping me from listening to the Spirit?

PART II

ACTIVATE YOUR FAITH

Faith Without Works Is Dead

CHAPTER III

MOVING FORWARD IN FAITH

"These people honor me with their lips, but their hearts are far from me.

They worship me in vain; their teachings are merely human rules."

-Matthew 15: 8-9

Now that you have put first things first by learning to pray daily and seeking the guidance of the Holy Spirit, you are ready to activate your faith. You are ready to move forward in God and live your fullest life. There are only a few things that you must remember. Keep in mind that this journey called life is God's story. It is not your story. Even though you might think that you should have the leading role because this is your life, you don't. Your life is controlled by God. Fortunately for us, God is an all-knowing and compassionate God. He knows the full picture of our lives—even the end at the beginning. He knows the stumbling blocks that will try to block us or detour us. He knows when to push us forward because His timing is always perfect.

When I first became a teacher, I thought I was good at what I did. After about five years, I thought I deserved to be the teacher of the year, but I didn't get the award year after year. That caused me to try harder and work at it even more. I kept trying to step up my game and get more and more proficient. After a few years, I completely forgot about being teacher of the year, but instead, as a Christian, my mindset became that of Colossians 3:23, and I began to practice doing everything with excellence and heartiness as unto God and not to man. Then to my complete surprise, during my thirtieth year of teaching, I was named Teacher of the Year at my school, and during my school luncheon to celebrate, I gave God credit by saying that it was God who empowered and enabled me to do my job daily. All praise and honor went to Him.

22

Thinking back, I realize that I really deserved the recognition then because I knew that it really was not me but God in me. He allowed me to receive all sorts of training, graduate degrees, and serve on various committees to become well-rounded at doing my job. Now the light of my life had shone on Him. His timing was perfect because He knew that my declaration would touch the lives of others. Had I gotten the recognition earlier, I would have thought I was good enough and would never have worked so hard to improve.

Another time God's timing was perfect was when my husband and I were making plans to build our dream house. It was going to be a huge two-story attention-getter with a mother-in-law suite for my parents. My dad totally opposed it, but I felt that since we were doing something so unselfish for my aging parents, I surely deserved some extra credit points with God. When we received preliminary approval, I just knew we were on our way, and soon we would have a big, fabulous house and be the envy of the family, neighborhood, and everyone. Then the news came that we did not get the final approval, and we would not be able to get the house. I was devastated. I took the contractor's sign down and burned it. I was mad at God. That was February, and six months later, the economy was in turmoil. The school year dropped from 180 days to 165 days to save money. I took a $10,000.00 drop in pay. My husband's job dropped to 4 days a week, and his salary dropped as well. Had we gotten that house, we most likely would have had serious financial difficulties and may have even lost the house.

To this day, we are still in the modest 3-bedroom, 2-bath house that we have raised five children in. We have done quite a bit of work on it, but I am happy to be in the comfort of a home that doesn't cause me sleepless nights. You see, God knew what was ahead, and He allowed us to not get approval for what we could not handle. He knew that we really did not need a new house and certainly not one that big. He knew that I really wanted it for show and that I could better serve my parents in other ways. Now we are basically empty nesters. Our present home is just the perfect size. We are free to enjoy life without financial struggles. We are living our best life.

God does not do anything just because. He is protective and intentional, and if we stay close, He will connect the dots for us. In time, we will see His hand at work. When I look back on those instances mentioned above of my life and so many others, I begin to see patterns of God's hand in my life. Satan has often tried to thwart and even kill my dreams, but when I have trusted the leading and the creativity of the Holy Spirit, even greater things have taken place. He has often sent me human messengers in personal conversations, through books, sermons, songs, other places, and even various social media platforms to encourage me to push through and not give in to fear, excuses, and procrastination.

Despite the differences in all our lives, there are seven basic steps to activate faith in your life. The life of Peter is a good one for observing these basic activation steps. Peter's walking on water has always energized me. You see, Jesus, who had spent several hours praying, crossed the mountain, and came walking on water to meet his disciples, who had gone ahead of him in a boat to the other side of the lake. At around 4:00 in the morning, it was still dark, and seeing what they thought was a ghost, the disciples were scared out of their minds. Jesus encouraged them not to be afraid because it was Him. In his typical impulsive way, Peter said Lord, if it is really you, allow me to come to You. Jesus said, come. So, Peter stepped out of the boat and began to walk towards Him, looking straight ahead at Jesus. Focused, Peter was walking on water! But as often happens to all of us, the distractions around him took away his focus, and he collapsed. Even so, he cried out, and Jesus saved him from drowning.

Yes, it is possible to do what seems impossible. For your life to be complete, connect the dots just as they have been orchestrated. Observe the examples of Jesus and Peter in Matthew 14. Ask God for what you desire, even the hard things, and then listen to hear his voice to do what He says. Focus on Him while you labor to move forward, but if you lose your focus, be quick to cry out to Jesus, who will never leave you or abandon you.

- Pray daily in all honesty about all things.

- Be obedient to Holy Spirit.

- Learn from your trials and errors.

- Observe the ways of God.

- Learn to apply the Word to your life.

- Be alert.

- Focus on God while you do the work.

Peter was brash, arrogant, and made mistakes, but He did the work He was called to, and when he focused on Christ, he literally walked on water. And so can you. Have the faith to do the work.

Questions to Ponder:

1. Am I focused on Christ or those around me?

2. Do I see how God is using everything in my life, even my worst tragedies, to propel me into His kingdom work?

3. What is holding me back?

CHAPTER IV

CALLED TO MINISTER

For many are called, but few are chosen.

-Matthew 22:14

The parable that Jesus gives in Matthew 22 regarding those offered to the wedding feast is quite profound and unsettling. Jesus tells the story of the King who has a huge banquet, and when it was time for the banquet, those who had invitations had excuses regarding why they could not come. They treated the King's servant badly, who bid them to come. The King sent the servant out to the countryside to invite all that were seen. As a result, at the appropriate time, the banquet hall was full. Then something surprising happened when the King joined the festivities. He saw a man with no wedding garments. The King had him bound and thrown out of the banquet. You are probably wondering what this story means and how does it relate here. The Jews represented those originally invited to the banquet. In other words, they were the ones who were meant to accept salvation through Jesus. When they refused Him, those others out and about (meaning all the Gentiles/all other peoples) were offered salvation. The one thrown out of the banquet for not having on the wedding garment represented those who give lip service to God but who have not accepted Christ in their heart. They are pretenders who only talk about their faith but do not really have any. Thus, the verse, "many are called, but few are chosen."

What is important here for you to know is that if you have truly accepted Christ into your heart and your life, you are not only called to the saved life but you are also chosen to minister to others in the kingdom. You may have been called to the ordained ministry as a minister, pastor, or priest of the gospel in a church setting. You may be an evangelist or prophet. But more than likely, you're a mom or dad, career person, businessperson, entrepreneur, or just a regular guy or girl. News flash! You are still called to minister. The Bible says, "you are the light of the world and the salt of the earth." That means you are God's advocate in the world. You are an example to others of how a chosen one lives. It is a privilege to be chosen to minister to the world, to be a prophet to the nations—a messenger of the gospel.

If you are going to activate your faith, you can't avoid your testimony. That means two things. First, you must have a test. Secondly, after you have proven to be an overcomer, you must use it to reach others. In Matthew 4, we see that the Spirit led Jesus into the wilderness to test Him. After 40 days of fasting, Jesus must have been tired and hungry, but God's Spirit strengthened his inner man. When the devil tried to get Jesus to err, Jesus quoted appropriate scripture to combat each temptation. Satan was not able to get Jesus to fail, and if we follow His example, we, too, will be able to pass the test given to us. And when we tell others how God helped us become a recovering drug addict or alcoholic, overcomer of abuse or molestation, conqueror of being a greedy materialist, a fake, or a phony, etc., then we can help others. We can say to them that if God did it for me, He can do it for you.

That is what it means to minister to others. There is an old hymn entitled, There is a Balm in Gilead. One verse says, "If you can't preach like Peter, if you can't pray like Paul, then tell the love of Jesus, and how He saved us all (AME Bicentennial Hymnal, 1984)." In other words, tell what you know about God. Tell how He saved and delivered you. Tell how you overcame the challenges you had and still have, with Jesus by your side. It is not necessary to be in any certain position in the church to minister to others. It is not even necessary to be in church. God needs believers in every aspect of society. He needs Christian men and women in businesses, the corporate world, academia, government, and all elements of society. He needs people on the streets, in the prisons, halfway houses, and on the mission field. He needs strong mothers and fathers to train up children in the ways and knowledge of God.

In Luke 19, a dreaded tax collector named Zacchaeus heard that Jesus was coming through town. He had heard a lot about this man Jesus and felt compelled to see him. He was a short man, and so he climbed a sycamore tree to see Jesus. As Jesus came by, He told Zacchaeus to come down because He was having dinner at Zacchaeus's house that evening. After time spent with Jesus at dinner, Zacchaeus's heart was changed, and he vowed to give back the money he had stolen as a tax collector because it is impossible to have an encounter with Jesus and remain the same. But the turning point of the story was when Zacchaeus was so desperate to see Jesus that he climbed the sycamore tree. We encounter desperate people who need to see Jesus and need help to see him. To them, we are a sycamore tree. We help them see the one with whom they can have a life-changing encounter.

Just as God had placed that sycamore tree in the right place for Zacchaeus's encounter with Jesus, he will place you in the right place to help someone in need. Your story of healing and deliverance will be a light to them. Your life is a sermon to them. Your test will become your testimony.

As you move through this life, you must activate your faith by helping someone else along the way. Your blessing will bless someone else. That is the whole concept of paying it forward. You thought it was a new concept, but God initiated the concept over 2000 years ago. He gave the mandate to help others and even made it known that you are blessed in order that you might bless the next man, and not so that you can hoard up resources and store them for some time when you might possibly need all that stuff. No, just as those in the wilderness could not save manna from one day to the next, we are to use what we have, and if we have more than we can use, the right thing to do is to share with the less fortunate. "Lord, give us this day our daily bread."

Share your resources, your love and respect, and your story. Know that unless you can articulate your own life story of how God delivered, protected, saved, and restored you, then you have not fully given your life over to Jesus, and you are no good to yourself or anyone else.

The Bible warns of those who pretend to be one way, but they are totally the opposite. Isaiah 29 talks about the judgment that will befall those who draw near with their mouths and honor God with their lips, but their hearts are far from Him. Remember, man looks on the outward appearance, but God looks at the heart. Whatever you do, keep it real. Keep your heart postured toward God to activate your faith.

Questions to Ponder:

1. Am I stuck in inactivity?

2. Can I identify a test that I have overcome?

3. As a conqueror, why aren't I sharing my story with others?

PART III

PREPARE YOUR LEGACY

Passing the Baton

CHAPTER V

BIGGER THAN YOU

Then Jesus told his disciples, "If anyone would come after me, let him deny himself and take up his cross and follow me.

-Matthew 16:24

During my participation in the Free of Me Bible Study facilitated by Dr. Sharon Hodde Miller (Free of Me Bible Study, 2018), I was reminded of how often in society we judge our worth by our appearance. Women are taught from an early age that their worth is measured by how pretty they are, how their hair looks, their body type, what they wear, and even more appearance-related features. The funny thing about that is that everyone has a different opinion about what looks good. So, the thing to do is not to play into this type of mindset. Rather than being overly obsessed about our appearance or even our possessions, we should put that time and energy into focusing more on God.

Jesus set the stage for us. He came to earth humbly and lived a modest life. His focus was on pleasing the Father and not on his own glory. Of course, we know that he wasn't interested in fame and fortune. He wasn't enamored by the kings, governors, and important people that He came before. Instead, He spoke truth to power. Remember His response to Pilate, who told Jesus to speak up for Himself because he had the power to kill him or let him go free. Jesus said that the only power Pilate had was that which His Father allowed him to have. Jesus used everything and every opportunity to bring glory and honor to His Father. Consider what Philippians 2:5-8 says:

"In your relationships with one another, have the same mindset as Christ Jesus: Who, being in very nature God, did not consider equality with God something to be used to his own advantage; rather, he made himself nothing by taking the very nature of a servant, being made in human likeness. And being found in appearance as a man, he humbled himself by becoming obedient to death—even death on a cross!"

Since Christ is our example, we must think like Him. We, too, should be more concerned with what brings Him glory and honor than the worldly thinking of "I've got to get mine." Christ knew that everything He did was bigger than what was happening right then. It was even bigger than Him. It was not just about Israel or those that lived right then. It was also about those to come and those after them. It was about countries and nations that did not exist at that time. It was not just about earth, but heaven on earth. And your life is the same. It is bigger, much bigger than you.

We live in a time when everyone is trying to be someone important. One of the most repeated statements made is for someone to declare that they are trying to be the best version of themselves. That sounds admirable, but the truth is that the statement is not what we should ascribe to. We should be trying to be more Christlike. You see, our focus is all wrong. We must start with the heart of a matter to make real and lasting change. That is what God is always after—the heart. The heart is the central focus. It is the essence of a thing. It is where the real belief lies. The Bible says that man looks at the outward appearance, but God looks at the heart. When we judge a man only by what we see, then we get a skewed look at that person. When we only show our outer selves to others, like most of us are prone to do on social media, then we can present a false picture of who we are. The point I am trying to make is that when we focus on ourselves and think that all of life is just about who we are and what we do or even if we include a few others in our view of the world, we are so missing the point of life.

You see, as we have stated before, God is intentional, and He is strategic. Nothing catches Him by surprise, and it is an honor that He includes us in the pages of history and allows us to make an impact. Acts 13:36 says that David died after he had done what God had for him to do in his lifespan. God has work for you to do——kingdom work that is specially mapped out for you. It is strategically placed for you in this space of time called your life, but it will impact more than just you, your family, and a few others you may encounter. Your purpose is bigger than that because it will impact life now and life in the new heaven on earth.

That is why you cannot just obsess over the small things like appearances and possessions. You have those things merely to use to maneuver in the lives of others and attract others to the kingdom of God. While the Proverbs 31 woman is lauded for beauty, charm, and how industrious she is, the most important thing about her is that she is a God-fearing woman. Those other things about her will all fade away.

God has a funny way of showing us what is important and exposing the lies we tell ourselves. When the pandemic closed the doors of my church, I told myself that I would start a podcast to present a Bible study lesson once a week, thinking that perhaps a few church members might tune in. A year later, after over 2000 downloads and listeners from all over the United States, Puerto Rico, France, and Russia, people are still listening to those pandemic episodes. God turned a small innocent project into a worldwide venture. I may not ever visit those places and witness to those people personally, but God made it possible for me to witness to them through technology without using advertisements, selling, or marketing. The church members passed the episodes to others who passed them on. I uploaded them to Apple podcasts, and the rest is history. Even now that I have stopped making new weekly episodes, surprisingly, people are still downloading the messages.

We must stop making decisions based on our intellect alone. We must be open to the Holy Spirit and His guidance. God knows everything and knows it before it happens. God knew that pandemic would happen, so he had me experimenting with various types of technology and taking courses on technology beforehand. I was confused by the leading to learn all those types of things until the COVID-19 Coronavirus showed up. Then I saw the need to know all this stuff and the purpose of it. However, I still did not envision the impact that simple 4–7-minute recordings would have. We just do not know all that God has in store for us. We don't know how big a deal it is to use the possessions God has given us. Everything we have has a purpose, and we need to listen to the Holy Spirit to guide us regarding how to use what we have, what He will allow us to acquire, and the people He will have to cross our paths—some of whom we will bless, and some will bless us.

We also need to realize that God has extended to us a way to touch the lives of many people in a powerful way without ever speaking to them. Sometimes we touch their lives without them ever knowing. We can even touch the lives of those who are unborn. Prayer is a powerful tool that we often discount, especially intercessory prayer.

We are called to cover each other in prayer. That means we should pray daily for our families, friends, church members, community members, and colleagues at work. When we know of specific issues and challenges they are having, we should address those in prayer. Sometimes we will not know specifics, but God has given us a prayer language to use. We are told to cover future descendants and those in our family that do not know the Lord. Before his conversion, Constantine's mother reportedly prayed for years for her son to receive salvation, and her prayers were answered. As the first Roman Emperor to claim Christianity, her converted son had a profound impact on the church and the expansion of Christianity to the Roman Empire and ultimately to the world.

In addition to those we know and love, we should pray for governmental officials, authority figures, and global partners. Pray for them to exercise Godly knowledge in their lives. Pray for the Holy Spirit's wisdom and guidance. Pray that God will show up in their lives and that they will accept Him into their hearts and their lives. And finally, God says that we must pray for our enemies. Listen to Matthew 5:44, 47-48:

"But I tell you, love your enemies and pray for those who persecute you... If you love those who love you, what reward will you get? And if you greet only your own people, what are you doing more than others? Do not even pagans do that? Be perfect, therefore, as your heavenly Father is perfect."

The point is that everything we do in this life for the kingdom of God is not about us alone, but it impacts hundreds, maybe thousands of others across many territories. It impacts generations now and many to come. It is so much bigger than you and me.

Questions to Ponder:

1. Do I know and understand what my kingdom work is?

2. What resources, gifts, talents, or opportunities has God granted me?

3. Am I using those things to advance God's kingdom?

CHAPTER VI

GLOBAL MINISTRY

He says: It is too small a thing for you to be my servant to restore the tribes of Jacob and bring back those of Israel I have kept.

I will also make you a light for the Gentiles.

-Isaiah 49:6

Growing up in South Georgia, in the sixties and seventies, I attended a church where everyone looked like me. Occasionally, I would see a congregation on TV with one person of color in a white setting or a Caucasian politician making the typical appearance to our church near election time. But most of the time, it was just us, an all-black congregation. So, when I started seeing totally mixed congregations on television and hearing about some locally, it really challenged me. I began to search my heart to know why it gave me a sense of uneasiness. After prayer and seeking God's wisdom, I realized that I was perpetuating the very same thing that the Israelites were judged for. They wanted to remain set apart, but not for Godly reasons. Instead, they wanted it for prideful reasons. I, too, was being prideful. I pondered the many meaningful relationships that I'd had over the years with people of other races and realized how ludicrous it was that I was being scornful of anyone attending our church or becoming a member of the body of Christ. We all have the breath of God inside of us.

The Israelites wanted a king to bring them back to the status among the nations they previously held when other nations feared them and showed them reverence. This was basically why many rejected Jesus. He did not look kingly, and he did not act in the manner that they perceived. Jesus had to correct them and say that He came to bring salvation to the entire world, to the Gentiles nations, and not just to the Jews. When I realized all that, my perspective changed, and then I began to question why more congregations do not have mixed worshippers. There is, of course, one Lord, one faith, one baptism. I realized that to not recognize that the Spirit of God can reside in all people of any race, ethnicity, or nationality is sheer ignorance or prejudice.

When we look at the Bible, the issue of race was never a factor. All peoples of the Bible saw each other as part of the human race. The problems between the nations came about because of territorialism, greed, style of worship, etc. Of course, the God of Israel was different from all the other gods, making the nation of Israel the target enemy of all the nations. But even at that, throughout Biblical history, God showed up in many ways and to many different people. He showed up to Abraham and led him away from his father's house to another land to become the father of many nations. God showed himself strong in the life of Ruth, who was a Moabite, to the nation of Nineveh after Jonah preached to them. He showed up to the Hebrew boys in Babylon and Daniel in Persia. He spoke through men who possessed all kinds of gifts and talents, such as Amos the farmer, Luke the doctor, Isaiah and Jeremiah the prophets, Solomon the king, Matthew the tax collector, and many others. He spoke through women, like Jesus' personal friends, Mary and Martha, Moses' mother Jochebed, Deborah the judge, Rahab the harlot, and Esther, the beauty queen. Jesus was born in Bethlehem, spent time as a baby in Egypt, traveled throughout the territory we now call the Middle East. He was born into the Roman Empire and spoke Aramaic, and His message went out to the Greek world because Alexander the Great had conquered much of the world. His disciples carried the message to the Gentile worlds—-Africa, Russia, and the like. And we still have missionaries who tread in uncivilized parts of the world today to carry the Gospel of Jesus Christ.

God is the originator of diversity. He made each of us different and chose different paths for us. He gave each of us a different fingerprint and different DNA. He loves all of us the same and expects, no, He demands, that we love each other the same.

God's desire is that all mankind would be reconciled to Him. That none would perish and that all would be saved. We realize that all men will not be saved because of free will and the fact that some will not accept the gift of salvation. But that does not negate the fact that all men have been offered salvation. It is the choice of each person.

So, we all know that Isaiah 49:6 sets the stage for the work of Jesus Christ. Jesus is coming to set things straight, not just for the Jews, the tribes of Jacob, but for the whole world. We, too, must think globally, beyond the four walls of the brick-and-mortar church, beyond our families and friends, beyond our acquaintances and countrymen. We must think of our enemies, those in undeveloped nations, those on the fringes of society, the outcasts, the disenfranchised, the abused, the hurt, and the voiceless. We must do our kingdom work with the mind of Christ, reaching out to our neighbor, whether he or she may be miles away, or our actual neighbor down the block, or across the tracks in that bad part of town.

As we reach out to all those around us, wherever we find ourselves and in whatever profession, business, arena, or circumstance, we are to be ready to leave a legacy of faith and a legacy of resources. When I say a legacy of faith, I am referring to the example we set by the work that we do. Kingdom work has a different look and feel from secular work. Kingdom work is done with the guidance of the Holy Spirit at the helm. It is always covered first and foremost with prayer at the beginning, middle, and end. Kingdom work is done not in our strength but of the strength of Almighty God. It is done with passion and in excellence. So, when others observe us and all we do, they see Christ. His handiwork is all over what we do and speak. They see that prayer is an integral part of our lives. They see that we do not take any credit but give God all the honor, glory, and praise. They see that our work gives us pleasure, and we do it with total awesomeness. And when we are overwhelmed, God makes us rest.

Not only do we leave that type of spiritual legacy behind as an example for others, but we also should steward all our resources in such a way that we have an inheritance to leave to our children. Just as David helped Solomon by gathering the materials needed to build the temple and Abraham left many riches and animals to Isaac, we should build wealth, not for us alone, but for those who come behind us that will make the next lap in the relay race of life. We must pass the baton in a clean, clear manner for success to occur.

My dad was not a rich man, but he was faithful to God. He often told us the story of how he and my mom struggled to make ends meet when they first got married. He drove a delivery truck, but they lived down a dirt road. When it rained, the road would get deep potholes in it. The owner of the company was concerned that the potholes would cause his truck to wear out, so he was on the lookout for my mom and dad to move to a different location away from the dirt road. He told my dad about a new house on a state highway nearby that was for sale. My dad laughed and said that he and mom would love the house, but they had no money to purchase it or even make a down payment. My dad said the man told him that he had a plan. He told my dad to ask his mom for $100, to have mom ask her parents for $100, and he would lend them

$100. Dad was to then present the homeowner with the $300 down payment for the house. If the owner sold Dad the house, the truck boss would give my dad a small raise. In return, my dad's boss would not have to worry about a damaged truck, as you might have guessed. The plan worked, and from those humble beginnings, my parents owned other houses and purchased many acres of land that have blessed their children and grandchildren.

Some of that property that they acquired allowed each of their children, me included, to become homeowners at an early age. Their resources blessed us in a big way, giving each of us a big advantage in life and the ability to do more to help our families, church family, and the community. Inherited wealth is a wonderful gift. The Bible talks about what a wealthy man Abraham was, so much so that three generations later, Jacob had enough wealth to attempt to give away a huge amount of stuff to make peace with his brother Esau, but we find out that Esau was wealthy as well. It all goes back to the inheritance of Abraham to his son Isaac and Isaac to Jacob. And along the way, each descendant acquired more to pass on.

We come to realize that both spiritual faith legacies and resource legacies advance the kingdom in a big way so that those who inherit those things can run faster and farther than the previous generation. If you are born into a family of believers, you have a foundation of faith and examples of faith that can aid in your growth. Granted, not all descendants of faithful men and women in the Bible turned out to be faithful themselves. I want to highlight Solomon, the son of David. When he became king, he prayed to God. He acknowledged the goodness and steadfastness that God had granted to his father, David. He said that now that he was king, he needed God to grant him the wisdom to govern the people. He wanted discernment to tell good from evil. Because he asked for wisdom, God granted him both wisdom and riches. How would Solomon have known to speak to God in that manner other than because his parents taught him? Even though David and his wife were not perfect parents, they knew God and had raised Solomon to be a child of God.

Do not ever think that the things you do will not affect your children and your children's children. The Bible refers to generations of things. Deuteronomy 5 talks about the iniquity of the father being a problem for the children for generations, but God is showing mercy to thousands who love Him and keep His commandments. It matters how you pass the baton to the next generation. You can pass Godly examples of faith that will inspire them and prayers that God will answer in their lifetime. You can leave them wealth that will jumpstart their life ministries in the kingdom, or you can curse them and cause them to begin life in struggle.

Questions to Ponder:

1. Do I see myself inspiring others around the world?

2. How am I stewarding the physical and spiritual resources I have now?

3. What would I like to be most remembered for?

PART IV

FOCUS ON GOD

Getting Unstuck

CHAPTER VII

ENJOYING JESUS

...for the joy of the Lord is your strength.

-Nehemiah 8:10

Now that you know how to pray, activate your faith, and leave a legacy, you are nearly done unlocking the path forward. There is one concept left to follow. That is focusing on God.

Are you a rule follower, or do you follow the basic practices of right and wrong? Jesus judged the Pharisees for following the letter of the law while ignoring the spirit of the law. For example, He spoke harshly to them for complaining about Him healing someone on the Sabbath Day. They were following the commandment of not doing any work on the Sabbath but had no compassion on the person who had been suffering for an exceptionally long time. The same kind of analogy goes for the person who follows the rules of spirituality but does not enjoy their saved life.

When I got my first car, I was so excited, but realizing what a big deal this was, I forgot to enjoy it. I would grip the steering wheel and watch out for everyone around me. I came to complete stops at intersections and waited a few seconds before pulling off at the green light. I was an absolute rule follower while driving my new car. I would not even turn on the radio most of the time, and driving with friends was an absolute negative since they might distract me. But I had a girlfriend with a car. She often invited three of us to ride with her. She drove with one hand and turned the radio on and louder when her favorite songs came on. She sang along, shared in the conversations of her passengers, even turning to face those she responded to. She drove through yellow lights just as they turned red and hardly noticed the other drivers around her. She enjoyed her car and driving it seemed to bring her sheer positive energy.

I wanted what she had with my car driving experience, so slowly, I began to think about the joy of driving and the blessing of having a car. I went from a nervous, uptight rule follower to a car owner who was thankful and blessed to enjoy my driving privileges. You see, I believe that is the way it is with many saved folks. Like the Pharisees, they are so caught up and anxious to keep all the rules of the saved life, including many that are only man-made additions to God's law that they simply do not enjoy life, and soon they fall away to do things that are totally ungodly.

Jesus showed us how to enjoy life the way God would have us to do it. He went to a wedding and even contributed to the celebration. When they ran out of wine, prompted by Mary, his godly mother, he turned barrels of water into wine. The celebrants remarked that traditionally the wedding party gave their best wine upfront, but in this case, the best wine came later. Of course, we know that Jesus never did anything in mediocrity.

Jesus visited his friends, he laughed and talked with his disciples, he fished, cooked, ate, cried, slept. He led a normal life, in addition to serving, healing, praying, preaching, teaching, and doing all the things we generally associate with the saved life.

I believe that if Jesus lived among us today, and I asked Him to, He would go with me to see a good movie (probably a G-rated one, though) and enjoy a cup of coffee with me in the mornings. He would like it if we went for a long walk, especially if we observed and appreciated nature. I think Jesus would try out some of my favorite recipes and enjoy eating at a good restaurant with me. I believe He would love to join in the conversations with my husband and me and laugh at some of the funny things that my grandchildren say. I even think Jesus would like to play a game of racquetball with me and watch LeBron James play basketball or Russell Wilson play football. And, of course, Jesus would love to hear Yolanda Adams sing. I believe Jesus would love those things because I love those things, and when I do those things, I feel close to God.

The saved life is one of freedom. The Bible says that he who the Son sets free is free indeed. We don't have to be rule followers. In fact, those who tried to follow the ten commandments found that it was impossible to do so. That is why Jesus came to set us free from the law of sin and death. Now, if we believe in Him, faith in Him alone grants us salvation. "For by grace, we are saved and not of works. It is the gift of God, through faith, so that no one can boast," as stated in Ephesians 2:8-9. Salvation is a gift of God. It is not by being a rule follower that we enjoy the saved life. It is by the work that Jesus did on the cross, by His death on the cross in our place, that we are able to take advantage of a blessed and full life.

So, what is stopping you from enjoying Jesus? Are you trying to follow something you were taught as a child? I was taught to keep a holy reverence for my Bible and never put it on the floor. When I really began to read and study the word, I wrote notes in my Bible, often went to sleep reading it, and slept with it on the floor under my bed. God has never called me on it.

Maybe your church has some peculiar distinctions that you think will give you extra credit with God, like saying various chants, dressing a particular way, or singing certain songs. The most important thing is not doing certain things to look holy. It is your heart posture that matters. God requires that your heart be yielded to Him and to doing what pleases Him, to be willing to put aside our goals and our agenda to do that which He is calling us to. If that is the case, then on your own, without having to be held under a set of laws and rules, you will do what is right and what is pleasing to Him, keeping in mind that God is always above man. What pleases God is always above what looks good in the eyes of man.

Enjoy the saved life. God made this earth for us. He never said He just wanted to spend time with us in church services or during Bible study. He wants to be a part of everything that is a part of our lives. He does not want to be separated out. There are mountains and beaches, rivers and ponds, trails, gardens, flowers, fishing, horseback riding, and the like. The earth is full of different types of jobs, people, entertainment, and activities. We can choose what we like to do and where we want to travel to and reside. The thing is, enjoy it all with Jesus. Give Him praise for creating it and making it available to us. Give Him the honor for allowing us to take part in it. Thank God for Jesus. Do not shut Him out or separate Him out by saying these are things I do with you, Jesus, and these are things just for me. Realize that if we are saved, we will enjoy eternal life. What do you think we will be doing with all that time? We will be doing the things we enjoy, and Jesus will be right there doing it with us. Let's start practicing that right now. Let our heart posture always be thank you, Jesus. I love you, Jesus. Let's do this!

Questions to Ponder:

1. What rules am I trying to follow that take away my joy?

2. Am I doing things that I know are ungodly and unpleasing to Jesus?

3. How would my life change if I included God in the everyday activities of my life?

CHAPTER VIII

NEVER GIVE UP

Weeping endures for the night,
But joy comes in the morning.
-Psalm 30:5

P. S. God never promised us an easy life, but He promised He would always be with us.

When three of our children were 11, 9, and 4 years old, my husband was scheduled for surgery to remove part of his large intestine and be given a temporary colostomy bag. A short time later, doctors were to do reconstructive surgery to reattach the parts of the large intestines and fix it to somehow eliminate body waste the usual way, without needing a colostomy bag. As complicated and sensitive as this all seemed, we were happy for him because it would mean a better quality of life. My husband had suffered for over ten years with an unidentified illness that mimicked both Crohn's disease and ulcerative colitis. He would have sudden urges to have a bowel movement without warning and literally had to run to the nearest bathroom. It happened all the time and became nerve-racking. We never went anywhere without knowing where there was a bathroom. We limited visits to some places and cut out many altogether. In addition to that, he would have countless bouts with severe stomach pain and suffered through periods of weight loss or weight gain from steroids that, in the end, were not effective. Through it all, he was a champ, rarely complaining but pushing forward.

So, when his Mayo Clinic doctors decided that he needed surgery, we agreed. I had gone with him to practically every doctor's appointment over the years and walked with him through the countless colonoscopies that in those years made him so sick that he always threw up. He had aches, pains, emergency room visits, and accidents in his clothes. We always traveled with extra clothes, no matter how short the time we would be away from the house. I would often wake up at night to find him moaning and groaning. I cried at night in the dark and prayed. But nothing prepared me for the feeling that I had as they wheeled him away down this long cold hallway, and he gave one last serious look at me over his shoulder. If I had not had a relationship with my Lord and Savior Jesus Christ, at that moment, I would have fallen apart—-gone completely mad. That is exactly what I wanted to do—to scream at the top of my lungs.

I felt completely let down. I thought in my heart of hearts that this might be the last time I would ever see my husband alive. What would I do without my best friend? How would I raise our children alone? This was not what I signed up for. How would my life go forward?

There comes a time, and if we live long enough, multiple times, in our lives, when we come to a reckoning. That was a day of reckoning for me because the Holy Spirit challenged me to believe what I was praying for, that my Darrell would live on, and we would continue life together. In my struggle with unbelief, I asked God how I could believe that he would be healed when others died from similar illnesses. How could I be so bold as to think it even possible? The answer came that I did not know or need to know why others may not have been spared, but I needed to pray in belief.

I remember sitting in the waiting room, thinking, praying, wanting to cry but refusing to let go. Surgery was to take several hours, but I was determined to wait it out. I was alone. Others who would have been there with me were taking care of the kids. I was alone with God, and suddenly there was a nurse. She said to go through the side door into a private room that the surgeon would come and talk to me. I was shocked. It was too soon. Something must have gone wrong. Before, I had wanted to scream. Now I just wanted to run away as fast as I could and just keep running. But I walked through the door as told, and the surgeon came in. What he said was incomprehensible. He said that when he had cut my husband open, his intestines looked basically nothing like what they had looked on all the x-rays and tests he had gone through. He said he poked around and checked all the other organs, and everything looked good. So... he said I sewed him back up.

Unbelievable! It was a miracle. The messed-up colon they were expecting to take out was in much better shape than they thought. The other organs were not affected, and my husband would live. God had answered my prayers, but not in the way that I thought. I asked the doctor, but what about his quality of life-changing. He basically said that however he had managed before, he would have to continue to rely on that.

As I look back and reflect on that time in my life, I see the goodness and graciousness of an understanding God. I was selfish, unbelieving, and ungrateful, but my heart was postured toward God, and so He guided me along the way until I was ready to handle more. My husband recovered from the surgery but continued to have problems. Three years later, he went back into surgery again. This time the colon was so deteriorated that the entire large intestine and part of the small had to be removed, leaving no possibility of reconstruction. My husband was left with an ileostomy and would have to permanently use a colostomy bag. In addition, cancer was found, and he would have to undergo chemotherapy. And I was four months pregnant.

This time the news was harder and heavier, but God had prepared me. I knew what to do. I prayed that God's Will be done in all our lives and that we would have grace each day for the hours before us. I prayed that the baby I carried would be strong. That my husband would be strong. That our other children would be strong. That I would be strong. And I knew that God would never fail me or abandon me—never leave me or forsake me.

No matter what hand life deals you, keep the faith. God knows all and has seen it all. Nothing catches Him by surprise. The troubles you have today may seem overwhelming, but years down the road, you may see them as pathways to a stronger, more faithful you. In the years and especially those trying moments of my husband's journey through illness, this is what God was accomplishing in me:

- I was being pruned.

- I was growing in my faith.

- I was being tested.

- I was getting stronger.

- I was gaining a testimony.

- I was yielding control of my life to God.

Sometimes we mistakenly think that being in God's Will means that we are shielded from the ills of this world. I have often declared that the safest place to be is in the Will of God. And subconsciously, if not overtly, I thought I was shielded from evil. While God protects us, we are not always kept from the tests and trials that come with living in a fallen world. When I went through the trials of the illnesses and surgeries of my husband, we both were in a solid place regarding our relationship with Christ. We knew Him, we loved Him, and we were serving Him. But that did not keep us from being stretched. Trials come to make you strong. In his song "Through It All," Andrae Crouch declared that if I never had a problem, I wouldn't know that God could solve it. I wouldn't know what faith in God could do, but through it all, through it all, I learned to trust in Jesus, I learned to trust in God. Through it all, through it all, I learned to depend upon His Word (Through It All, 1995)."

Never give up on God. Whether you are in bondage, in a pit, or just in a holding pattern, know that God will show up. Life is beautiful, life is full, life is hard, but life is never dull. Keep praying, activating your faith, preparing your legacy, focusing on God, and you will live a life of purpose blessed by God.

Questions to Ponder:

1. What stage of my spiritual life am I in now?

2. Have I learned to deal with the challenges of life, or am I still in a fog about where God is taking me?

3. Can I identity the pitfalls and stumbling blocks that keep me bound?

4. What is Holy Spirit saying to me about where I go from here?

Personal Notes

REFERENCES

- AME Bicentennial Hymnal. Nashville: AME Publishing House, 1984.

- Crouch, Andrae. Through It All, 1995.

- Lucado, Max. Grace for the Moment. Nashville: HarperCollins Christian Publishing, Inc., 2007.

- Miller, Sharon Hodde. Free of Me Bible Study, RightNow Media, 2018.

- Nicole, Rameesha. Healed Trauma = Healed Finances Challenge, 2021.

- Towns, Elmer L. Theology for Today. Belmont, CA: Wadsworth/ Thomson Learning, 2002.

Made in United States
Orlando, FL
09 September 2022

22241623R00029